ALAN SHAPIRO

Reel to Reel

THE UNIVERSITY OF CHICAGO PRESS

Chicago & London

ALAN SHAPIRO has published 11 books of poetry, most recently *Night of the Republic*, a finalist for both the National Book Award and the Griffin Prize, and *Old War*, winner of the Ambassador Book Award. He teaches at the University of North Carolina at Chapel Hill.

The University of Chicago Press, Chicago 60637
The University of Chicago Press, Ltd., London
© 2014 by The University of Chicago
All rights reserved. Published 2014.
Printed in the United States of America
23 22 21 20 19 18 17 16 15 14   1 2 3 4 5

ISBN-13: 978-0-226-11063-9 (paper)
ISBN-13: 978-0-226-11077-6 (e-book)
DOI: 10.7208/chicago/9780226110776.001.0001

Library of Congress Cataloging-in-Publication Data
Shapiro, Alan, 1952–
    [Poems. Selections]
    Reel to reel / Alan Shapiro.
        pages cm—(Phoenix poets)
    ISBN 978-0-226-11063-9 (pbk. : alk. paper)
    ISBN 978-0-226-11077-6 (e-book)
    I. Title. II. Series: Phoenix poets.
PS3569.H338A6 2014
811'.54—dc23

                    2013016631

♾ This paper meets the requirements of ANSI/NISO Z39.48-1992 (Permanence of Paper).

Thirty Years of
PHOENIX POETS

Reel to Reel

for TOM SLEIGH

CONTENTS

ACKNOWLEDGMENTS

Grateful acknowledgment is due the editors of the following
magazines and journals, where some of these poems first appeared:

Atlantic Monthly: "Wave"
At Length: "Homeric Turns"
Cortland Review: "Dialogue" and "Emissary"
Greensboro Review: "Taung Child"
New Ohio Review: "Beach Towel" and "Open Door"
The New Yorker: "Reel to Reel"
Plume: "On Thumbing through *Smith's Recognizable Patterns of
    Human Malformation*"
Provincetown Magazine: "Thought Experiment" and "The Not Lord"
Slate: "Wherever My Dead Go When I'm Not Remembering Them"
Virginia Quarterly Review: "Gravity" and "In Winter"

One

WHEREVER MY DEAD GO WHEN I'M NOT REMEMBERING THEM

Not gone, not here, a fern trace in the stone
of living tissue it can somehow flourish from;
or the dried up channel and the absent current;
or maybe it's like a subway passenger
on a platform in a dim lit station late
at night between trains, after the trains have stopped—
ahead only the faintest rumbling of
the last one disappearing, and behind
the dark you're looking down for any hint
of light—where is it? why won't it come? you
wandering now along the yellow line,
restless, not knowing who you are, or even
where until you see it, there it is,
approaching, and you hurry to the spot
you don't know how you know is marked
for you, and you alone, as the door slides open
into your being once again my father,
my sister or brother, as if nothing's changed,
as if to be known were the destination.
Where are we going? What are we doing here?
you don't ask, you don't notice the blur of stations
we're racing past, the others out there watching
in the dim light, baffled,
who for a moment thought the train was theirs.

REEL TO REEL

Passed on to me after my brother's death,
My name in marker on the see-through plastic
Of the giant reel, on which the melody

But not the words of "Jeepers Creepers" breaks off
Halfway across the bridge into my voice
At nine, with two friends on the tape, three boys,

Three voices on the tape, three high-pitched in-
Distinguishable voices hamming it up
Together on some day I can't remember

In a far corner of the playroom where
My brother every evening sang the words
While the tape recorder played the melody,

Every evening no matter how tired he was,
No matter what else he needed to be doing,
Or wanted to do, despite the pleas, the sulks,

The tantrums, because he had a gift, she said,
And, fine, if he didn't want to honor it, fine,
His choice, he could kiss it goodbye, for all she cared,

But one day he'll realize what he's lost, one day
He'll wish he'd listened to her—one day, that one
Day each day shaken at him like a club.

Which voice is mine? Who's there with me? What's left
Of that day, of any day of all those years
In the cramped house: two reels, one thin, one fat,

And brown tape threaded through the housing, which,
When you hit RECORD, sounded (if you said nothing)
Like water rushing far off underground,

Turning the reels too slow to ever see
The thin one fatten or the fat one thin.
And "Jeepers Creepers"—that was his specialty,

His show stopper, what he always opened with,
Her little Mel Tormé, her Buddy Greco,
So cute, so sexless, she could eat him up,

When he was on stage: the adorable red blazer
With bright white piping on the lapel, white pants,
White patent leather tap shoes, straw hat, and cane.

I see him when I hear the melody,
And somehow I hear every word he sang,
But not him singing on those evenings half

A century away, no single one
Of which I can remember anymore.
"Where'd you get those peepers, jeepers creepers,

Where'd you get those eyes" that hated me
Every evening as they couldn't not
Because I didn't have a voice or gift

To be alone inside the spotlight of,
No fear of any day that lay in wait
To make me sorry. "Gosh oh git up

How'd they get so lit up . . . how'd they get that size . . ."
The slow reels changed without appearing to.
"Woe, woe, woe is me, got to get my cheaters on"

The moment when the tune breaks into nothing,
No words, no music, the hush a sound of water
Rushing underground, until a boy

Laughs while two others wrestle for the mic,
And then all three are laughing, hamming it up—
"Heavens to Mergatroid!" "A wise guy, hey!"

Just that, those seconds, "gosh oh gee oh," just
The voices of a ghostly slapstick now
From reel to reel to ferry us across.

THE FAMILY BED

My sister first and then my brother woke
Inside the house they dreamed, and so the dream
House, which, in my dream, was the house in which
I found them now, was vanishing as they woke,
Was swallowing itself the way the picture did
Inside the switched off television screen.
It was the nightmare picture of them sleeping
As if alive beside me in the last
Room left to us, the nightmare of the picture
Suddenly collapsing on the screen
Into the tick and crackle of the shriveling
Abyss they were being sucked away into
By having wakened, while I, alone now,
Clung to the screen of sleeping in the not
Yet undreamt bedroom they no longer dreamed.

WAVE

Of and not of
water, moving in water
through it
while the water lifts in place
as it passes
buoy and boat, the way hands
in one row
rise as one to fall
as the next
row rises, in a phantom
billowing of
and not of, in and other
than, across
the stadium, over the bed
in the flapped
sheet rippling as it's drifting down.

Sine and swerving cosine
of the starling
cloud, of the shock waves
of the bomb blast,
of the slithering snake or the snaking
river which somehow
is the same shape as the building pressure
of the urge of
the desire in the middle of which

the air, too,
atom by atom, rises and falls
with the cries cried
at the same time from your lips to my ear,
and from mine to yours.

THE GATE

There in the last before
of early late,
when our bodies become both garden
and unlocked gate,

both the children playing hard
and the game they play,
so lost in playing that
they couldn't say

what turns in the sensation
of sensation turning
from long and slow—just when?—
to sudden burning,

burning in taste and touch
so thoroughly
that my skin tastes of you,
and yours of me—

and taste is scent and scent
is everywhere
enveloping us like
an atmosphere

of briefest having that
we can't believe
up to its breathless end
will ever leave

until it does, and in
the dark we find
the children we thought we were
left far behind—

back in the garden while,
beyond the gate
that's gone as soon as entered,
soon shrinks to late,

and play to pulse receding
to withdrawn kiss
to garden bed now just
the bed it is.

AGING LOVERS

Shaking the chill
off starts with you
pretending not
to know I watch you
while I watch you
pretending not to,
in the lamp-lit
twilight we prefer,
that we can both
half hide in—
because it suits
what sags, what shrinks,
and leaves us free
to think I'm watching
you be watched
by me in secret
as you unbutton
now and now un-
hook untie let
slip so non-
chalantly I
can hardly stand it
while I pretend
I can because
that's how it quickens
in you to the

shimmying out
of and the sliding
off and down
to only shadows
falling all
around bare skin
that though goose-
fleshed and shivering
won't be rushed, no,
it just takes longer
at this stage
to shake it off,
the chill, the change,
the sudden cold
front heightening
the heat it meets
at last under
the covers I
am lifting up.

THE CAVE

Imagine the electric
Air ways
Suddenly visible,
All of them
Everywhere like
Neurons firing
Kaleidoscopically
In air, the empty
Air we move
And breathe in
Crosshatched now
And crisscrossed
Like a planetary
Nervous system
Passing through
The very bodies it
Began as, as if
There were no bodies,
Every hate and
Love cry of the body
Old and young,
Long dead and dying,
Scribbling their lightning
Urgencies at once
In all directions
In an inverse

Of the parable where
Inside is outside,
And lights are shadows
Of us flashing at us
Over bright
Cave walls of air.

THOUGHT EXPERIMENT

Your face as an unbroken
line of moments
reaching back from
old to young to
unrecalled and
unrecallable
beginnings—your face
at any and every
moment all along
that daisy-chain
of faces changing
even while each face
is bordered by
identical versions
of itself—the
transient sameness
of the face before
and after just a
slower kind of
cloud drift
ever young
till not, and never
old till old,
improbably
as hand from paw

from wing from fin
("How? When?") day by
indistinguishable day.

ON THUMBING THROUGH *SMITH'S RECOGNIZABLE PATTERNS OF HUMAN MALFORMATION*

to Annie Dillard

And what of the bird-headed dwarfs
on page 657, the naked boy
and girl in a bleak light
on a shameless table, propped up
side by side by a single hand,
by a thumb and finger?

What of the boy's chest, or the girl's,
no wider than a deck of cards,
each face no longer than a thumb?
What of the normal eyes
made huge by the shrunken
features? Or the wick-

like legs they cannot
straighten, the twisted arms,
the smile as sweet as any
that only the girl
is smiling, still too young
to get it, as she holds her arms up

high as if for an embrace
and not because she had been told to
for the picture for the textbook
so we can see them better,
smiling as if pretending so
could make it so,

while the older boy, who gets it,
his mouth like crimped thread,
grimacing, as he looks away,
won't look into the camera—
looking away as from
a small unpleasantness

he grudgingly gives in to
for his own good,
though he can't see how
or why, the helpless
rageful dignity of looking
elsewhere, as if it were

the body only, and not
him caught naked
there on page 657
of the 1000-page book,
unhoused, unhouseled
on a metal table, in the blameless

wrong of a design he gets,
he gets it, if not all the time
and everywhere, then there
and then, when the camera flashes
fixing him inside the isn't
of what everyone else is,

which is why he isn't
smiling like his sister, no,
not now, not here, not
even if asked to, he won't

be like the other smiling
children in the book,

who smile like children
even while being spit
out onto the page by what
beyond the page outside
the book is deeply
drinking all the others in.

TAUNG CHILD

What led you down, first mother, from the good
dark of the canopy, and then beyond it?
What scarcity or new scent drew you out
that day into the vertical-hating flatness
of the bright veldt, alone, or too far from
the fringes of the group of other mothers
following the fathers out among the herds
and solitary grazers, the child clinging to your back
when the noiseless wing flash lifted him
away into the shocked light as the others ran?
Two million years ago, and yet what comes
to me, in time-lapse through cascading chains
of changing bodies, is not the tiny skull
I'm holding, not the clawed out eye sockets,
his fractured jaw, but you, old mother, just then
in that Ur-moment of his being gone,
what I've felt too, on crowded streets, in malls,
if only briefly, in the instant when
the child beside me who was just there

                                        isn't

before he is again, that shock, that panic,
that chemical echo of your screaming voice.

GRAVITY

Pervasive ghostly
whatnot of the
felt invisible
streaming back
and forth of mass-
less particles that
anything with mass
reels out of itself
to reel in whatever's
smaller (how, by
what means, pulling
with what, or
pressing?) along
lines of force
in fields of
force that lessen
never quite
to nothing over
infinite distances,
at all times, in all
directions where
there's no direction
and even light is
sucked like a body
into the densest
hole of it, or curls,

photon by photon,
at its horizon like
a flock of starlings—
and in the dream
vision of its utter
opposite—which is
not grace—you are
the object only,
the merely acted
on, subjected
to, dumb thing
at rest, in nothing,
nowhere, im-
moveable, or moved
so continuously
forward at the
same speed it's
the same as rest—
it is the nightmare
of the absence of
all sense of this
way or that or
fast or slow, which
suddenly you
wake from, falling
without time
enough to reach
for anything
between what's rushing
from you and
what's rushing up.

IN WINTER

Broad leaves of bittersweet enveloping the dead
and dying trees, flourishing up the trunks
and out across the lower branches to
the few abandoned nests they haven't yet
invaded: every leaf now almost seeming
to signal something to no one about the never
to be disentangled moment of itself,
how all their surfaces flash and go dim
all morning, in and out of focus, too bright,
too dark, too suddenly or slowly now
in ever varying miniscule degrees
of sun and shade too subtle to be named
changing before my eyes across what also
changes before my eyes without my seeing,
like the bloated carcass of the squirrel
caught in a crook of branches, bloated, seething
with little scavengers that carried it
away in sun and shadow as it shrank
invisibly to nothing but this flattened
wisp of dark between the flashing leaves.
Leaves signaling about it, whether they are or not,
something about what can't be thought about,
impenetrable, irreducible,
as the recurring no time of the ice
you dream between you and an open door
you cannot enter, where the ones you come for,

look for, and even think you see inside it
looking out, are looking out, but not
at you, and only briefly, from a dark
that all at once is darker for the ice
that flashes up so brightly that it blinds.

DISASTER MOVIES

Why can't he look away as it gathers toward him
Down the long avenue, that giant wave
That rises high as the high rises to break
Over the tiny multitude that scatter before it,
Or the absolute zero of the snow blast
Shriveling bodies instantly to crystal,
Or oceans sizzling as the asteroid falls,
The postapocalyptic sleep walk of
The lucky ones in a gray silt of air,
Himself among them stumbling over rubble,
Searching for wife or child, and then not searching?
Is it preemptive terror that he wants,
Feeding the fear of the unthinkable,
Till he can somehow think it without fear,
Or is it something else, some kind of jubilant
Impersonal yearning for complete release,
So deep inside him it is outside too,
A yearning using him to think about itself,
Thinking itself in rippling aftershocks,
Collapses, or the way now sudden rain
Spills over the gutters like molten glass,
A billowy pane of glass that blurs the trees
To tree-like vapor, and the vapor sways
And runs, and everywhere the sound of running
Is the sound of everything released from the
Magnetic strain of being what it is,

Him most of all, losing himself inside it,
Far away and near, and loud and soft,
In through the window as a faint cool prickling
Too fine to wet the skin, too damp to dry it off.

BEACH TOWEL

Imagine sitting on some towels on a beach,
and suddenly it's raining, and you scramble up,
hurrying over the sand with all the towels
to a stall inside the bathhouse where
the towel you choose to dry yourself off with
is only a little dryer than you are,
and then, as you continue drying, isn't,
it's wet too, too wet, wetting as much as drying.
You pick another towel up but it's
damp too, in fact they all are, every one
as wet as you are, towel and skin
exchanging the same dampness—if the bath-
house door were open you could run outside
into the sun and dry yourself, or find
another towel and pass the wetness on
in a one-way trade off of damp for dry.
But now imagine that the doors are locked,
the stall door and the bathhouse door, and you,
you can't get out, you have only these towels,
you can't escape these towels, you can't get new ones,
there's no way to make one thing go one way or
another: imagine energy as dampness,
the jiggling accidents of energy
spread out like dampness over everything
so evenly that there is nothing left
of any kind of more of this for less

of that to balance or redress, no one
to help or call to, nobody else to touch:
Now picture everyone locked up with you,
each in his own stall, having waited there
so long inside that chilly damp enclosure
that the world beyond it may as well not exist,
or ever have existed, and you're all shivering
in the cold air, but since no warmth remains,
there is no shivering, nobody is there.

LAW OF MOTION

On his last day, more baffled than afraid,

more curious than baffled, all Jack could do

was watch us like a child in a new place,

seeing as for the first time how we moved

around the bed, about the room, tracking

the moment by moment shifting mesh of shade

and light across this hand, or that face as

it brightened almost into recognition—

into and out of the cloudy opalescence

he watched all day, he studied like a child

inside a speeding car, who can't connect

the motion outside with the stillness in—

amazed, if also baffled and afraid,

beneath a flickering mesh of shade

and light that's sliding over what trembles

under it, beyond the window, trembling

with the force of everything

that's rushing all around his being

so very still inside the car.

ABSOLUTE ZERO

Is called "the death of matter,"
which must mean that matter,
no matter how dead, if
it could get this cold,
would then be even deader.
And if that's true, then is
"the life of matter"
before that cold is reached
the way the matter moves
within itself, its "warmth"
a measure of the subatomic
traces of that movement,
so that when there isn't
any colder to be gotten to,
it isn't that the matter
disappears so much as that
it doesn't, that it's just there,
too there unchangeably
inside itself to be itself,
transformed by being locked
into an at-attention in-
attention nothing at that
temperature could break?

The temperature was falling
inside the room around
the bed, past speech, past
twitch or eye blink, falling
into absolute aphasia,
Ultima Thule of effacement,
falling while I held on to the dry
ice of the hand, the chilling
matter of it, dead and yet
continuing to die, as if there were
no end to the getting
colder, to the falling into
merely being there beyond
the black moon of the sunless
galaxy at the outer reaches
of what I couldn't reach
or release inside the hand
that took heat from my hand
and would not warm.

YOU

No center or
circumference to
the circle of
yourself, beyond
which there is
nothing which
isn't also
you—preceder
of the past, surpasser
of the future, and in
between, if not you,
then your every
moment of an arrow
passing through us
till we fall and it flies
beyond us into
more of us.
Who else but you,
cold maker of the vastly
small within an outer
space so vast
that any distance,
however great,
compared with it,
is just as small—who else,
freak spawn of utter

emptiness, could have
performed there in a
father's eyes now eyes
no longer such
an absolute and
instantaneous alchemy
in reverse, taking
back into yourself
what out of yourself
you brought forth
by increments so slow
and artful that we can't
help think of it
as love? Who else
but you compels
this crying out
to you from deep
inside the soundless
vacuum of your
being where
nothing can be
heard at all?

EMISSARY

Out on the very edge
of the farthest inkling
of beyond, beyond
the background echo
of the gone beginning,
at the heat death
of the last bit
shivering back
into the nothing
it had been before
before proliferating
out in an accidental
chain of causal
chains of particles
swirling mindlessly
to dis- and re-
combine through eons
after eons
into the minds
composed of particles
that told the story
of the journey out
of nothing back to nothing
across the pages
of a book high on a shelf
in a library long since

disassembled into
what at the end
will be our only
emissary—that
final trace, our boatman
made of the ghostly
stuff he ferries, of the boat
too and the black water
that isn't water,
or boat or boatman
rowing to no shore.

DIALOGUE

If the abyss alone surrounds us,

Bounds us

Comes out of everywhere to find us,

Remind us

Of what we can neither think about

Nor live without

The thought of, how then do we live?

We live

Day after day, we sleep we wake

We make

Do with what we do until we don't.

Or won't

So what will leave me when I die?

I

And what will replace me in this place?

Space

But if that's true then what can matter?

Matter

But how did I get from that to this?

Miraculous

Random swirl of particles

That chills

And burns in an ever-changing state

Indeterminate

In every way but in the making

Unmaking

Of what it is, then isn't, here

Or there

In each unlikely curl and angle—

Angel

Of no thought thinking itself through us,

Dust

We cling to, kill for, deplore or yearn,

Urn

Of nothing and to nothing prey—

Pray

For something more than bleak repose

That knows

Not much given to us to trust to

Must do.

Two

HOMERIC TURNS

I.

Consider it all as two songs, ours and theirs,
And theirs composed of one high note, too high
For us to hear, and played so constantly, so
Uninterruptedly that they themselves
No longer hear it, if they ever could.
And ours, its crooked passage up and down
The scale of feeling, unforeseen and fated,
Note vanishing as soon as played, and played
By vanishing into the song it is—
How could it not astound them, air, just air
Resisting air, inflected with the sound
Of never-enough, and too-soon, and if-only—
Brief shapes of air between the silences
Only the song articulates by breaking.
And so imagine: it wasn't the husband blundering
In and snatching the baby from the flames
That could have saved him, but the mother-goddess,
The glistening one herself, who held her hand
Against the heel pad, and the pliant tendon,
The skin the fire would cure now soft as ether—
An ether nearly anything could tear.
Touching the tiny foot she felt afraid,
And liked the feeling. And though the baby kicked
And kicked to feel the fire all over him,

43

Kicking with all his might to get free
As the flames rose, she only smiled at his strength
And gripped him tighter and would not let go.

2.

The gods laugh, that's what they're good at, laughing.
They laugh at the crippled god, his shriveled legs,
His hobbling, and his mother, in a little
Shadow play of suffering at the sight of him,
Her crippled baby laughs the loudest, and then
Laughs even louder when she hurls him out
Of heaven, and he falls, and while he falls
The laughter echoing around him is
The measure of the pure unbreathable cold
Height of the heaven he's falling from and through,
Hilarity of light and air, delight's
Effacement of everything but itself.
And the crippled baby tumbling to earth
In a charade of terror? Don't let him
Deceive you—he's a god—he's laughing too.

3.

The sodium streetlights down the avenue
Were vague globes where the dark turned orange,
And the orange dark. The avenue deserted,
The buildings all abandoned, or soon to be,
I drove, I can't remember where, or when,
Though it was late, or early, and the night
Was heaviness my headlights had to push
Through slowly, till I passed a side street where
I saw two figures fighting, two men, one pummeling
The other against the hood of a parked car.
A woman nearby screamed, for God's sake, stop!
And suddenly the hero of the story,
God-crazed with justice, without thinking, I
Slammed on the breaks and, running hard to throw
Myself between them, shouted, Hey, Hey, Hey,
Suddenly bigger and stronger than I was.

Well, that's the story, anyway. In the one
I'd later come to tell about what happened,
I don't exactly say that I was fearless,
Or even that I ran to help; I say
Instead I walked as slowly as I could
And hoped with every step the guy would stop
Before I got there. I smile then, sheepishly,
As if to say I know it isn't right
To seem too much the hero of a story.
It makes a better story if you're not,
And thus makes you a better hero. And so
I then say when I got there I discovered

It wasn't a fight at all but only shadows
The street light threw down through a wind-swept tree
Against the car hood, and no woman screamed,
Although, in truth, she did, or might have, I don't know
Really, I couldn't say if she was there,
Or not, it was so late, after all, or early,
In the orange darkness of a strange
Dark city I was lost in, and besides
My heart was pounding so hard as I drove past
I couldn't tell you what it was I saw.

4.

What if they got it wrong, the tribe of singers,
And none of it was true: she never sailed
In the benched ships, she never went to Troy,
And there had been no bed befouled, no god-bound
Slaughterhouse of honor to be sung about?
What if the unsung were the only song,
The simile reversed, the rank and file
Massed for a sleep walk into corpse fires just
A figure now for storm clouds out at sea,
The storm itself a storm and nothing else,
Whipping great breakers onto breakers till
Even miles inland from his mountain top
The goatherd sees it turning day to midnight,
Summer to winter, sees it and shivers, driving
The flock before him to a cave where, safe
And dry now, he can watch the fabulous black
Sky crazed with lightning till the storm has passed.

5.

Hers were the bright veils of disclosures of
What shines by hiding, the no sooner here
Than gone sensation of desire dis-
Entangled from desire and cut loose
As mist about the body, in the heart,
The sight of her a dazzling emptiness
He swirled another mist around, gold mist
Inside of mist, a swirling doorlessness
That nothing but itself could penetrate.
And there inside it, the about to have
And having, and the having had of sleep
All flashed at once like different facets of
The single shining of the thing it was.

We've known it too, for moments, you and I,
Each in our own way, together, or with others,
Enclosed, and drifting, arrogant as gods
Who in the gold mist of that complete forgetting
Forget that in the killing fields below
Their shining sons, the fretted over, doomed
Swift Runner, Wily, Breaker of Horses, all
Cry out for them to bless the sword they raise
Against each other, to bless the hacking down,
The butchering, the dragging in the dust,
Not knowing that their parents aren't their parents now,
Now they've never been parents, they have no children,
The only cry they're hearing is their own.

6.

Murmur of house flies in the window where
The twisted strips hung softening in the heat,
Swaying and trembling as the stuck flies, slimed
And furious, struggled across an inch wide desert.
Some were caught by both feet while the wings whirred
And buzzed as the body tried to lift free of
What wouldn't let it. And some with one wing caught,
The other whirring, could only sideways slide
And crawl around itself against itself
Over and over in a ragged circle,
Sliding and crawling till it finally stopped.
But the ones I watched most were the strongest ones,
The most determined, who would fight free of
The paper and then below it on the sill,
With forefeet glued together, and still wet
With glue, for hours would mop the gummed head with
The very gum it tried to mop away.
Sometimes I'd pencil a circle around one and
Then come back later to see if he got clean
And got away. But no one ever did,
Or if he did he only got an inch
Or so beyond the tiny winner's circle
Of my attention before I'd brush him off
Into the pile of the other once great fighters
Filling the trough between the sill and pane.

7.

Because she was his mother and a god,
Even down at the bottom of the sea
She could hear him crying, sprawled in the dust
Before the body of his friend. Because she was
His mother, she could cry and beat her breast;
But because she was a god too, she could rise
As water out of water onto the shore
Where she could cradle him, his godlike head,
The way a mother would, to soothe but not
To save him, no, not that, because, more god
Than mother, trapped in flawlessness, she was
The glistening one, who glistened even then
Among her sisters who like sisters came with her
To cry as only they could cry whose names were
Mist and Fair-isle, Down-from-the-cliffs, First Light,
Bright Spray, Bather of Meadows, Eyes of the World.

8.

The ocean's river circles the great shield's rim.
Inside it is a field, a vineyard, vine poles
Weighed down with gold grapes ripening like grapes,
Each dew wet cluster soon to be stripped and crushed,
Forever soon to be, here where they climb forever,
And down the one footpath the pickers run,
Their wicker baskets swinging by their sides,
Young girls and boys, all running to the field,
And in the midst of them a child is singing,
Plucking such clear notes from a golden lyre
That the gold air all around him, could it hear him,
Playing and singing dirges for the dying
Where nothing dies, even that air would long
To be the air it isn't, if it could long.

9.

The wave is building as it approaches shore,
Out of itself upon itself, the long
Back steepening with shine until the crest
Curls over and breaks, exploding into spray
Against the backwash of the wave before it—
Earth shaker, steadily, day and night, the surf
Pounds on the shore and, in the suck and drag,
Takes back a little of it, grain by grain,
In time lapse plundering that in its own
Time, soon, will have it all back, beach and salt
Marsh, river basin, and the rising plain—
The ancient citadel itself now less
than the collateral damage of a moment,
crushed in the giant down beat of its crashing
into the silt the idiot force will carry
over the earth and into it and out
again, ten thousand years away, beside
another ocean in another field
where an old man sees two white stones propping up
a tree stump, not rotten through by rain,
and wonders if it's the start or finish line
of a forgotten track, or just its half
way marker, or the last trace of a grave mound
of a hero dead too long to be remembered.

10.

Suburban Homer, not suburban hero,
all I can tell of it now is night and walking
into and out of dark between the halos
of streetlights down a dark-bright avenue.
Where was I going, furious and afraid,
hurrying from what had happened, which, because
I could not say it, wouldn't stop happening
inside me, like some undeserved but longed for
violence or violation I needed
to get out of myself so as to quiet
the total infant hunger of the sound
of it inside me screaming to get out?

The solace I was after was an afterlife,
humiliations of the body burned
away in the fiery headlights to a name
on every grief struck tongue inside a house
my absence fills more than my presence could,
each one repeating versions of what now
they tell themselves they should have seen the signs
of all along, imagining (if they had)
the many ways they would have loved me better.

No one knew more about reality
or truth or honest speech than I did then.
It was the telling of what I couldn't tell
and couldn't not that told itself all night
in every furious footstep down that dark-
bright avenue, in every halo I walked

under and out of, and in every self-
entombing dream of loved ones dreaming me
after the funeral, dreaming I've come home
at last, come to the door they rush to open,
all so thankful so relieved to see me
that there's no need to tell them anything,
the story teller now the hero silent
among the cries of welcoming that only
my being dead enable me to hear.

II.

After the son dies, or the father, or the friend,
And the corpse fires all burn out; after the smoke,
The visible stench, so pleasing to the gods,
Has risen to the gods who send it back as black
Confetti, raining what began as men
Today upon the men who will tomorrow
Honor them by making more of them;
After the play hunt and the play kill of
The funeral games, and the sacrifice and feast,
When the watch fires gutter and go out and the whole
Field blackens into outer space—it's then
And only then that even the most enraged
Can sleeping find a refuge from his name,
And for a little while the name drifts free
Of epithet and set piece into a sound
No one is making. Think of a schoolroom between
Class when a teacher wipes the blackboard clean
And claps the two erasers and releases
The disarticulated powder of
A day of rules—think how they float now, the words
The men are made of, while the armies sleep
By the wine dark sea till the rosy-fingered dawn
Between books, before the page is turned.

Three

THE BRIDGE

Over the bridge across the river,
the pilgrims prayed in lockstep,
and the deafening coherence
of the single voice they made
was a fulfillment of the dream
each voice, alone, inaudible,
dreamt it could be as it prayed.

The gold dome of the holy shrine
beyond the bridge was glistening
like the paradise inside the prayer,
which the prayer was promising
to those who said the prayer
the way it wanted to be said,
which was the way they said it,

as if they were a people only
of the prayer, a people
spoken through by what
they spoke together, who
by being spoken through
could almost think that they
were there already—there

in the light of what they'd be
the single voice of endlessly
instead of merely people on a bridge,
instead of more and still more
jammed hard together, pressed
in and pushing in to inch
in forward like a giant knot

they were all trying to untie
by tying tighter under sun
that smoldered a white
hole in the dome's reflection
in the dark fast river—till
one by one all along the bridge
they started spilling over

like small impurities the praying
mass they were spit out
as it surged through and past
the screams that sank like duff
down the smoldering hole
the sun burned on the rippling
dome within the water

that outside the prayer was in-
escapable, uncrossable
except as water flowing from
and to within and over
water—made from water
out of heat forged from the
coldest nothing that there is.

POLITICS

At the bar they had no business going to
because of where it was, which was, of course,
precisely why she wanted them to go there,
he argued with her about their being there,
all through the first set and the second set
of the "real" blues they'd come to hear.

Her justice he called tyranny
of sympathy, her goodness, self-abasement,
and her refusal not to be aware
of other people's misery—Oh how
he'd like, just once, to tell her this—wasn't
it incidental to the finicky need
she had to be aware of misery,
suffering that need because she didn't
suffer enough to satisfy the need,
denying what would otherwise delight her
in punishment for privileges that made her
less than others for having made her more?

Oh he could see through it all, all right,
the goody two-shoed grimness of her outrage,
the circular urgency about his lack
of agency, how his refusal to act
was just as much an action as her refusal
not to—and later after they'd left and lost

their way at 2:00 a.m. on a side street,
he could see the charade, the scam, unfold
like a bad plot, as someone, a panhandler
(had he been drinking?) suddenly kneeled before her,
rag in one hand, spray bottle in the other,
and sprayed her boots and buffed them while she stood
there, looking down, and smiled uncomfortably
like a benevolent queen a little too
close to a subject:
                              I know where you got those boots,
I bet I know where you got those boots,
I may not know the store but I know where
you got them.
                    Okay, so tell me.
                                        You got them on your feet.

And when the man stood and put his hand out, laughing,
what could she do but laugh and give him what
she had, shaking her head, always the good sport,
although he noticed how her hand was trembling
when she took his and how it trembled as
they walked away, a little faster now,
and kept on trembling even while she tried
to laugh the whole thing off, laughing as if
to keep inside her hand what she allowed
only her hand to feel.
                            And if her trembling
hand relieved him of the need to say
I told you so, so he could simply be there,
walking with her, hand in hand, her ally,
her comforter, protector, didn't it also show

how brave the laughter was, how good, how decent—
and for a moment there it was, he could see it,
couldn't he, hiding right where it always hid,
right there behind the truth of his position,
what he felt

        too little of, too rarely,
more often than he ever cared to think.

ANGEL

In movies when they appear disguised as mumbling
schizoids or soiled drunks, junkies, the drooling
mongoloids, the stroke-addled baby-steppers,
the camera catches their angelic pedigree
by how the eyes flash or the lips curl up
divinely in a smile that only you,
outside the story, watching it, can see.
Outside the story, on the street, in the alley
between the car lot and the movie theater,
you found him in a sticky pool of beer
and vomit, walled in stench, bleary-eyed,
and shouting, "Shit on you" as you, because
there was no other way, stepped over him,
head turned, eyes watering, and as you passed,
again he shouted, "Shit on you," but now
in the dank air it almost sounded like
a joyful noise, an angry hallelujah,
as if delighted to have found you there
at last, you as you were, as you couldn't not
be just then as you walked away too quickly,
still hearing him, your Gabriel, your messenger,
just as he was, whether he was or not.

THE OPEN DOOR

for Peggy Rabb

What did it mean when she said at last, "All day
I have been running to the open door"—
What door was it she ran to, opening to what?
From what? And did she reach it and get through?

No one was there with her, it seems, inside or out,
No one she mentioned, no solving light or phantoms
Calling in parental voices, urging her
To come, child, run, and that she ran "all day"—

Was that the joy of being able now
To run in some way none of us could see,
A bodiless release imagining a body
If only to feel how free of it she was?

Or was it desperate running, running to
Get out of the nightmare room that was all day
Uncrossable, the door like a horizon
A stride away with every stride she took?

And if she reached it, running, what did it feel like
Then, that moment, being nothing but
The motion of herself without herself,
Over that threshold into nothing else?

GRACE

Grace, you told me once,
Would be a garden fenced
With singing only those
Inside could comprehend.

A garden dense with songs
That those outside it sense
As far off bird cries fading
Back into silences,

While voices inside weave
Through voices through the air
Of an unchanging key
Of being newly there

Where you too are, now, Wil,
If anybody is,
Your voice somewhere inside it
Lost in choruses

That I, from where I stand,
Forgive me, can't hear at all,
Your garden for me less
A garden than a black hole

No light, no song, no sounds
Of any kind escape,
Though I keep listening, friend,
If only for your sake.

SPOOKY ACTION AT A DISTANCE

She was crafted by the light
Of being looked at
By the someone
She imagined looking at her
When he would look at her.

He was happy to be
That someone, whoever he was,
Crafted in a play
Of lights (like color
From partial absences
Of light), so he
Could be, for once,
The kind of man who
Makes a woman
Look at him that way.

The airy lights
Of the precise conditions
Of her being able
To be looked at only
In the way she wanted
Reshaped themselves
Kaleidoscopically around
The little helpless, momentary
Failures of his looking,

So that it almost seemed,
No matter what he did,
He could do nothing
To displease her, and the

Shadowy figures
Beyond the light,
The ineptitudes,
The sniggering
Voices, the see-
Through masquerades
Of sacrifice—
What were they
But the chronic
Tricks of where
There was no light
Between them
To be seen through?

PHANTOM

I woke to the rustling upsweep of the covers,
And you whispering in sleep, come here,
Lie down beside me, lifting the covers higher
To the empty air.

Everything's okay, you said, don't be afraid,
Raising the covers like a wing
Of welcome to the ghostly hovering
Your dream had made.

And though I shivered in the sudden chill
Of tenderness so freely offered
To what could only be a phantom lover
I lay there still—

Caught in a giving colder than your own,
Unable to pull you close again
Till you could finally bring the covers down
And draw him in.

SAINT CHRISTOPHER

Mid-river, sunk in shadow, the saint
who doesn't know he is a saint
bends under the weight
of the child he doesn't know
is Jesus. He's reaching back
awkwardly with one hand
to shift the weight, secure his
grip, his head down, eyes
squinting with the strain.
He cannot see
the halo over the child.
He cannot see the angels
over the halo. The divinity
you see so clearly, that is
the very center of the picture,
is to him only a wrong
weight on his back, too
great for the little body
bending him over the
reflection of his bending,
which if he sees at all
must show him nothing
but what he cannot bear
as he bears it trembling,
step by step, across the river.

WHATEVER ELSE THEY'RE SINGING

Here now to me, this
moment waking, to
my ear, inside it,
echoing down
the fly ways ancient
even then so long
ago—high up
above the giant crater
and its pluming ash,
through ash rain, past
volcanic fires on their way
to me, to my ear, over
bogs and tar pits bubbling
where their last kin,
kin no longer, sink
in silence as their singing
passes, raucous,
joyful, over breaking
land mass, over land mass
sifting down, crushed under
sea floor into fire rising
out of water steaming
into land again—past
ice floe calving, over
cave, hut, house,
the killing fields,

the blinking towers, down
to me, my ear, this moment
singing, if nothing else,
that they are here and will be,
long after I am not.

SCATTER

my ashes on a night like this,
in a place like this, in the half dark
up high among the swallows.
And let the swallows feeding
as they slash and swerve
mistake the cloud of me
dispersing for an unresisting
richness, a lucky find,
so I can drift a while
in the wings' calligraphic
nonsense no less
jubilant for being so.
And the first fireflies
below me, let them each
come out of hiding.
Let them flash for once
in safety in the open air,
in praise or not, aware or not
but flashing freely through the dark
that I alone could draw
the fear from for a brief time,
fooling the swallows as I fell.

SUN

You cool by burning into light that blinds.
From surface down to center, out to in,
your heat grows ever hotter toward the core,
at once contracting as it gets heavier
and pushing out as it gets hotter, poised
between collapsing and exploding by
the massive quivering of your rage for both.
You are the massless bits we see you by,
the origin and end of seeing, the
without which nothing, which, some day, it's said,
you too will be, you dumb enlightener,
you senseless giver of sense that some of us
still pray to foolishly for all the gifts
you accidentally pour down over us—
impartially enough for us to call
you good, and long enough for us to say
you live forever like a god when what
we mean by that is how we aren't, and don't.

THE NOT LORD

"And him who escapes from the sword of Hazael
shall Jehu slay; and him who escapes from the
sword of Jehu shall Elisha slay."

The tribes, the states,
the multitudes of nations,
peoples to be slaughtered,
more numberless than all
the houseflies ever
to have died, the prophet's
prophecies banging
in the name of,
against a too clear
pane of: he who is
who he is, who
made the wind shatter
the rock face into rubble
but was not the wind,
who made the earth
shake open but was not
the earth, and not
the fire shaken
from the earth that,
after the fire, disintegrated
into vapor into air,
into the airy nowhere

of a quantum silence
inside the spectral
vagaries within
a vacuum of a
bubble of the not lord
soundlessly exploding
in the prophet's mouth,
on the prophet's tongue,
shaping the sounds of
what would happen soon.